Fact Finders®

MILITARY HEROES

THE TUSKEGEE AIRMEN

Freedom Flyers of World War II

BY BRYNN BAKER

CAPSTONE PRESS
a capstone imprint

Fact Finders Books are published by Capstone Press,
1710 Roe Crest Drive, North Mankato, Minnesota 56003
www.capstonepub.com

Copyright © 2016 by Capstone Press, a Capstone imprint. All rights reserved. No part of this publication may be reproduced in whole or in part, or stored in a retrieval system, or transmitted in any form or by any means, electronic, mechanical, photocopying, recording, or otherwise, without written permission of the publisher.

Library of Congress Cataloging-in-Publication Data
Baker, Brynn.
  Tuskegee Airmen : freedom flyers of World War II / by Brynn Baker.
      pages cm.—(Fact finders. Military heroes)
  Includes bibliographical references and index.
  Summary: "Discusses the heroic actions and experiences of the Tuskegee Airmen and the impact they made during times of war or conflict"—Provided by publisher.
  Audience: Grades 4–6.
  ISBN 978-1-4914-4839-7 (library binding)
  ISBN 978-1-4914-4907-3 (paperback)
  ISBN 978-1-4914-4925-7 (eBook PDF)

1. World War, 1939–1945—Participation, African American—Juvenile literature. 2. United States. Army Air Forces. Fighter Squadron, 99th—History—Juvenile literature. 3. African American air pilots—History—Juvenile literature. 4. African American air pilots—Biography—Juvenile literature. 5. World War, 1939–1945—Aerial operations, American—Juvenile literature. 6. Tuskegee Army Air Field (Ala.)—Juvenile literature. 7. World War, 1939–1945—Regimental histories—United States—Juvenile literature. I. Title.

D810.N4B35 2015
940.54'4973—dc23

2015017100

Editorial Credits
Editor: Jennifer Loomis
Designer: Veronica Scott
Media Researcher: Eric Gohl
Production Specialist: Tori Abraham

Photo Credits
Alamy: World History Archive, 24; Capstone: 12; Corbis: Bettmann, 13; Getty Images: FPG, 16, Gabriel Benzur, 18, 19, 23, Hulton Archive, 25, Win McNamee, 27; Library of Congress: 9; National Archives and Records Administration: 5, 21; National Museum of the US Air Force: 11, 14; Newscom: akg-images, cover, 20, 22, Everett Collection, 7
Design Elements: Shutterstock

Primary Source Bibliography
Pages 7, 18, 19, 21, 22, and 23—Homan, Lynn M. and Thomas Reilly. *Black Knights: The Story of the Tuskegee Airmen*. Gretna, La.: Pelican Publishing Company, Inc., 2001.
Page 11—Peters, Raymond Eugene and Clinton M. Arnold. *Black Americans in Aviation*. San Diego: Neyenesch Printers, 1975.
Page 26—"Honor thy Father: A Tuskegee Airman." http://www.josephgomer.com. Retrieved June 2, 2015.

TABLE OF CONTENTS

Chapter 1
WORLD WAR II HITS AMERICA 4

Chapter 2
PREJUDICE IN THE MILITARY 6

Chapter 3
***FAITHFUL* FLYERS** 10

Chapter 4
CIVILIAN PILOTS 12

Chapter 5
ARMY PILOTS 18

Chapter 6
TUSKEGEE AIRMEN 22

TIMELINE 28
CRITICAL THINKING USING THE COMMON CORE 29
GLOSSARY 30
READ MORE 31
INTERNET SITES 31
INDEX 32

CHAPTER 1

WORLD WAR II HITS AMERICA

World War II (1939–1945) was truly a global war. It spread across 30 countries and involved more than 100 million people. It was also one of the deadliest conflicts in human history. By the time it was over, an estimated 60 million people had died.

World War II officially began in early September 1939. It was then that Adolf Hitler led Germany's **Nazi** Army in an invasion of Poland. The Nazis continued their invasion across Europe, brutally murdering more than 11 million people, including **Jews** and other ethnic groups. This mass killing of civilians by Nazi Germany became known as the Holocaust. By 1941 the Nazis had conquered and were in control of most of Europe.

At the same time, Japan controlled most of Asia and was at war with China. The United States wanted to stop the Japanese but resisted getting involved in the war. Instead, together with Great Britain and the Netherlands, the United States **froze** Japanese assets, or items of value. As a result, Japan could no longer buy oil and fuel. Hoping to further weaken Japan's military, the United States also stopped exporting steel and iron to them. Japan's response was to form an **alliance** with Germany.

On December 7, 1941, the Japanese attacked the U.S. Navy at Pearl Harbor in Hawaii. More than 2,400 Americans died. The following day President Franklin D. Roosevelt declared war on Japan. Three days later, on December 11, President Roosevelt declared war on Germany.

During World War II, countries formed military alliances that became very powerful. The two opposing alliances were the Allies and the Axis powers. The Allies included the United States, Great Britain, France, and Russia. The main countries of the Axis powers were Germany, Japan, and Italy.

During the attack on Pearl Harbor, the battleship USS *Arizona* was hit four times by Japanese bombers. The number of people who died on board the ship was almost half of the total number of deaths that resulted from the attack.

Nazi—a member of the political group that ruled Germany from 1933 to 1945
Jew—someone who is descended from the ancient Hebrew tribes of Israel
froze—prevented the act of spending money or the withdrawal or exchange of something
alliance—an agreement between nations or groups of people to work together

CHAPTER 2
Prejudice in the Military

After Pearl Harbor was attacked, the United States needed the help of as many **recruits** as possible. African-Americans wanted the chance to help defend their country. Thousands went to recruiting stations to sign up for the fight. However, the military, like much of the United States, was **segregated**. Black men were not allowed to serve in the same **regiments** as white men. A limit was also placed on the number of blacks that could join the army and navy. Those who were allowed to join served in segregated regiments or worked as cooks and janitors on military bases.

The United States also needed combat pilots to help fight in the war. Much of World War II was fought in the skies above Europe. Pilots would be needed to fly fighter jets and bomber planes.

Many qualified African-American men volunteered to fly for the Army Air Corps. They experienced even more difficulty than the black men who volunteered for the army and navy. All Army Air Corps applications submitted by black men were rejected. Many military leaders believed blacks were not physically or mentally fit to fly.

recruit—a new member of the armed forces
segregate—to keep people of different races apart in schools and other public places
regiment—a large group of soldiers who fight together as a unit

President Roosevelt asked all Americans to help win the war in any way they could. Even after this call for help, African-Americans who wanted to fight for their country were treated unfairly by a racist military. This unfair treatment only strengthened black people's determination to be treated equally to whites.

During Wold War II, many African-American soldiers were given service positions, such as removing trash. These jobs required a lot of hard, physical work but little responsibility. Most black soldiers were never placed in active combat roles.

"I have applied at several recruiting stations at various times . . . for enlistment in the Army Air Corps, only to have been refused . . . on the ground that I am a Negro . . . I appeal to you for aid in securing the right to serve in the Army Air Corps without discrimination because of my color."

—Roderick Williams, a licensed black pilot, appealing to President Roosevelt in a letter after the attack on Pearl Harbor

African-Americans were disappointed in their country. The United States was fighting against **racism** in other countries, yet it ignored its own problems with racism. Black leaders decided to fight a "double war." In addition to fighting the Axis powers, they would also fight racism at home and around the world. At the same time, they were determined to prove they were just as qualified to be soldiers, pilots, and anything else, as white people.

A Segregated Society

During World War II, segregation was widely accepted as a normal part of U.S. society. African-Americans were often treated unfairly and denied basic opportunities. For example, blacks had to use separate and **inferior** facilities. They were required to eat at different restaurants from whites, shop at different stores, attend different schools, and even use different toilets. African-Americans also had to sit at the back of buses and were pressured not to vote in elections. Some blacks were even kidnapped and murdered for expressing their opinions or standing up for themselves. Extreme white racists tried to create fear in the African-American community and keep blacks "in their place."

Segregation was legally enforced in most U.S. states from the 1880s to the 1960s. The most common types of laws forced business owners to keep black and white people separate. For example, in Alabama it was against the law for black and white people to eat in the same restaurant unless there was a separate entrance for each race. Black and white customers also had to be separated by a solid wall or screen that was no shorter than 7 feet (2.1 meters) tall.

racism—the belief that one race is better than another race
inferior—lower in rank or status

CHAPTER 3
Faithful Flyers

Even before the attack on Pearl Harbor, African-Americans were fighting for equal treatment in the military. Dale White and Chauncey Spencer were two experienced African-American pilots. In 1939 they managed to collect enough money to rent a run-down plane that they named *Old Faithful*. The plane had no lights, brakes, or instruments to help them fly! Even so, the men planned to fly it more than 3,000 miles (4,828 kilometers) to prove themselves as pilots.

White and Spencer took off from Chicago on May 9, 1939. Along the way they faced many unexpected challenges. When *Old Faithful* had engine trouble over Ohio, the pilots managed a bumpy landing in a farmer's field. They installed some new parts and continued on to Morgantown, West Virginia. However, the white crew at Morgantown's airport refused to allow the black pilots to park their plane overnight. The crew told them to refuel and leave.

Next, White and Spencer managed to follow a much larger plane to an airport in Pittsburgh, Pennsylvania. But they were immediately **grounded** for violating safety regulations meant to keep planes from colliding. Black politicians and the legal team of the *Pittsburgh Courier*—one of the nation's top black newspapers—stepped in to help. With their aid, the charges were eventually dropped.

White and Spencer knew the importance of their journey, and through it all, they never gave up. They eventually landed in Washington, D.C., where they met Senator Harry S. Truman. He was impressed by the men's story and asked if they had applied to the Army Air Corps. The pilots explained that African-American applicants were always rejected. Truman seemed surprised and then asked to see *Old Faithful*. "If you had guts enough to fly this thing to Washington, I've got guts enough to see that you get what you are asking," Truman said. Truman soon sponsored a bill allowing black pilots to serve in the Civilian Pilot Training Program (CPTP).

Chauncey Spencer was born in Lynchburg, Virginia, in 1906. After completing college he wanted to take flying lessons but could not find anyone willing to teach him in Lynchburg. Spencer was able to receive lessons in Chicago where he worked at a restaurant. He used most of his earnings for flying lessons.

ground—to restrict the activity of someone or something

CHAPTER 4
Civilian Pilots

The CPTP began in many U.S. colleges in 1939. Its purpose was to train civilians to become pilots. In the late 1930s, the U.S. Army only had about 4,000 pilots. Many more would be needed if the United States entered the war. But at the time, the army wasn't large enough to train all of these pilots. The CPTP was the solution to this problem.

More than 1,000 colleges and nearly 1,500 flight schools participated in the program. The training was divided into 72 hours of ground-school classes and 35–50 hours of actual flight instruction. At the end of the program's first year, more than 9,000 military pilots had been trained. Thanks to Senator Truman, the CPTP became available to students at Tuskegee Institute beginning in December 1939. Tuskegee Institute was a highly respected black college in Tuskegee, Alabama.

Tuskegee Institute, now known as Tuskegee University, is located in eastern Alabama. It is the only college in the United States that is also a National Historic Site.

Tuskegee Institute was one of the first six black colleges to offer the CPTP. About half of the 2,000 black pilots who graduated from the program trained at Tuskegee Institute. The CPTP ended in 1946.

This partial victory was a huge step for African-Americans. They saw the CPTP as a way for them to eventually be allowed into the Army Air Corps. They hoped it would only be a matter of time before the U.S. military allowed black pilots to fly.

All CPTP students were required to take a written examination. In March 1940 the exam was given to Tuskegee Institute's CPTP students. Every student passed. Their passing rate was the best in the South.

Flying with the First Lady

Charles Alfred "Chief" Anderson was in charge of Tuskegee Institute's basic flight training. He taught hundreds of African-American students how to fly and was a hero to many. In 1941 First Lady Eleanor Roosevelt visited Tuskegee Institute. When Anderson took Roosevelt flying, she was so impressed with his skill and charm that she became a strong supporter of African-American aviation.

In 1932 Charles A. Anderson became the first African-American to receive a commercial pilot's certificate.

African-American Organizations

African-American newspapers, such as the *Pittsburgh Courier* and *Chicago Defender*, demanded that blacks be accepted as military pilots. They also requested that the entire military be desegregated. African-American organizations and politicians believed in the success of a united military and nation. The National Association for the Advancement of Colored People (NAACP) had made equal opportunity in the military one of its most important goals. They believed if African-Americans were allowed to fight in the military as equals, they would soon be treated as equals in all aspects of life.

But many U.S. military officials believed black people were inferior to whites and would only hurt the military. Even the white leaders who agreed with the demands still said they could not change society. However, African-Americans refused to give up, and they continued to fight for their rights.

Did You Know?

White officers in favor of allowing black pilots into the military were often told to keep quiet. Some were even moved out of their positions of authority.

The *Courier* Fights for Social Equality

Robert Vann, editor of the *Pittsburgh Courier*, was a powerful man with powerful friends. He worked hard to convince the military to admit black pilots. In 1938 he published "Ten Cardinal Points for Army and Navy Equality," stating that African-Americans deserve equal treatment and recognition.

The 10 Points:

1. We deserve jobs in the services.

2. We pay for jobs in the services.

3. Our fighting record should be rewarded.

4. We seek the test to prove our merit.

5. We need education just as the whites.

6. We seek the chance to shatter prejudice.

7. Our loyalty is an American tradition.

8. Americanism is [the] test of our fighting men.

9. We want to glorify America before the world.

10. We want to inspire future Black America.

In the 1930s the *Pittsburgh Courier* was one of the most popular black newspapers in the country. The newspaper's journalists called attention to problems many black people faced, including poor housing and limited health and education resources.

CHAPTER 5

Army Pilots

The U.S. military faced increasing pressure from African-American organizations to accept blacks as military pilots. On January 16, 1941, the U.S. War Department announced that an all-black **squadron** would be created within the Army Air Corps. However, they made it clear that black and white pilots and crews would remain segregated. "Segregation is an established American custom," explained Army Chief of Staff General George C. Marshall. "Experiments within the army in the evolution of social problems are **fraught** with danger to efficiency, discipline, and **morale**." Many members of the military thought that black pilots would not be able to perform well in combat. The training of an African-American squadron was considered to be an experiment that would fail.

At first, flight instructors who taught basic and advanced flight training at Tuskegee Institute were all white. Black instructors eventually taught there as well.

The 99th Fighter Squadron

Hundreds of African-American men volunteered for the new squadron. All volunteers had to take army intelligence tests. Most of the men were highly qualified college and CPTP graduates. Still, military officials were surprised so many did well on the exams. Top-scoring applicants moved on to Tuskegee Institute for five weeks of advanced flight training with the Army Air Corps. The men who successfully completed the training would become pilots in the U.S. Army. The training was difficult, but the black volunteers were more than ready for the challenge.

"We'd all go down to the flying lines ... and stand before our instructors," said Aviator **Cadet** Louis Purnell. "The instructors would come out and tell you ... 'We are going up to 10,000 feet, and we'll perform loops and slow rolls.' You'd wait your turn, then you'd go up. Instructors would say very little during instruction, but they were very strict. When you came down there was no exchange of words. He had a little slip and so many errors would amount to a pink slip." If a cadet got three pink slips, he was dropped from the flight program.

squadron—an official military unit
fraught—full of something bad or unwanted
morale—a person or group's feelings or state of mind
cadet—a military student

On March 7, 1942, the first class of African-American pilots at Tuskegee Institute completed their advanced pilot training. Cadet Benjamin O. Davis Jr. was among this remarkable group of men. Davis was a graduate of West Point, a well-known military academy in New York. After earning his wings, Davis was first promoted to captain. On August 22, 1942, he became **commander** of the 99th Fighter Squadron—the first black flying unit in the American military. Additional squadrons formed as more pilots completed training. These men eventually became known as the Tuskegee Airmen.

Benjamin O. Davis Jr.

Benjamin O. Davis Jr. was the only black cadet at West Point during his four years there. His fellow cadets refused to speak to him or share a room with him simply because of the color of his skin. However, racial discrimination never stopped Davis from achieving his goals. He continued to earn promotions throughout his career. In 1998 Davis became a four-star general—the military's highest rank during peacetime.

More than 2,000 African-Americans completed training at Tuskegee Institute during the early 1940s. They studied hard and hoped to finally join the Army Air Corps, but they were *still* rejected. "Applications from colored persons for flying cadet appointment or for enlistment in the air corps are not being accepted," said Major General E. S. Adams of the U.S. War Department.

> 3475th Q. M. Trk Co.
> Fort Ord Calif.
> November 10, 1942
>
> Mr. William H. Hastie
>
> Dear Sir:
>
> It has been several months since we have passed the necessary examination and approval of the Cadet Examining Board to qualify as an aviation Cadet.
>
> During the Course of our examination we were stationed at Fort Sill, Okla, at which time several other soldiers took the examinations and have since then received their transfers to the Air Corp; but for some unknown reason we have not received ours.
>
> Sir, we are college men and have had Senior R.O.T.C. training. We were also members of the Enlisted Reserve Corp. Since completing our basic training in Field Artillery we have been transferred to Fort Ord California to do basic training in the Quartermaster Corp. It seems, sir, as if we are going from one basic training to another and getting no nearer to the Air Corp. We are writing you hoping you may be able to give us either and or information so as to hasten our transfer to the Air Corp. It seems with aviation playing the vital part it is we should have hardly any trouble getting in. Our papers are in Washington awaiting disposition, as is the case of all Negro applicants. We hope you can help us. We close now awaiting your answer.
>
> Respectfully,
>
> Pvt. Rufus R. Johnson 15317492
> Pvt. Emory A. James 15317509
> Pvt. Jack Housen 15317527

William H. Hastie served as civilian aide to Secretary of War Henry L. Stimson from 1941 to 1943. On January 15, 1943, Hastie voluntarily quit his position to protest segregation and discrimination in the U.S. Armed Forces. Hastie, an African-American, became judge of the Third United States Circuit Court of Appeals in 1949. At the time, this was the highest court position an African-American ever held.

commander—a person who leads a group of people in the armed forces

CHAPTER 6
Tuskegee Airmen

By early 1943 the Tuskegee Airmen were ready and awaiting orders. The war raged across Europe and into North Africa, yet the black pilots were not sent into action. The U.S. Army held out, hoping more white recruits would become pilots. Meanwhile, the Tuskegee Airmen continued training and flew practice drills every day. At a flight show, Commander Davis told a crowd of people that his black pilots were performing as well as white pilots. "My greatest desire is to lead this squadron to victory against the enemy."

For training purposes the Tuskegee Airmen used an aircraft model called the Vultee BT-13 Valiant. The rear cockpit had a curtain that could block student pilots' vision. This forced them to rely only on the aircraft's five basic instruments.

In April 1943 the Tuskegee Airmen finally got the order they had been waiting for. They were shipping out to North Africa. They journeyed across the Atlantic Ocean with 3,400 white troops before arriving at their base in Morocco.

In June the Tuskegee Airmen got their first taste of combat when 12 German fighter planes were spotted off the coast of Italy. Six black pilots flying P-40 fighter planes circled above as the Germans fired machine guns. It wasn't long before additional German fighter planes showed up. The Tuskegee Airmen were seriously outnumbered, but their bravery and preparation led to victory. According to the mission's official report, "One enemy aircraft was last seen at 1,800 feet excessively smoking." Commander Davis' report stated, "It was the first time any of them had ever shot at the enemy. They gave a good account of themselves considering the odds ... and most importantly, they all came back safely."

Some Tuskegee Airmen noticed a bond between black and white Army Air Corps pilots. The white men who did the actual fighting and flying generally respected the Tuskegee Airmen as fellow soldiers and pilots.

Red Tail Angels

The 99th Fighter Squadron joined the 332nd Fighter Group in 1944. This group was made up of the 100th, the 301st, and the 302nd squadrons of Tuskegee Airmen. The 332nd painted its plane tails bright red, which earned the group the nickname Red Tail Angels. German pilots both feared and respected the pilots of the 332nd. They called them *Schwartze Vogelmenschen*, or "Black Birdmen."

Benjamin O. Davis Jr. eventually became the commander of the 332nd Fighter Group. He named his red-tailed plane *By Request* because white pilots would request Tuskegee Airmen to escort them on bombing missions. The pilots knew the Tuskegee-trained men were the best at protecting bomber planes.

The Tuskegee Airmen went on to fly more than 1,500 combat missions in North Africa, Italy, and Germany. They destroyed hundreds of enemy planes and successfully escorted more than 200 bombers. These bulky, slow bomber planes were easy targets for enemy attack. The small and quick fighter planes protected the bombers during missions. Many Tuskegee Airmen were awarded Distinguished Flying Crosses, Purple Hearts, and countless other honors for bravery and service.

Colonel Benjamin O. Davis Jr. (left) received a Distinguished Flying Cross in 1944 for escorting bomber planes. The man pinning the medal to Davis Jr. is his father, Benjamin O. Davis Sr., who was the first African-American general in the U.S. Army.

Fun Fact:

In 2008 the Tuskegee Airmen National Historic Site opened in Tuskegee, Alabama. The site's purpose is to honor the Tuskegee Airmen's heroic actions during World War II. Visitors to the site can see where the men trained and some of the planes they flew.

The Tuskegee Airmen played an important role during World War II. They helped the United States free Europe and win the war overseas in June 1945. But their most important victory was the one at home. These men showed a rare form of courage as they battled racism in the military. Their dignity in the face of cruelty inspired America to change. In fact, Harry S. Truman, who became president in 1945, desegregated the U.S. military in 1948. It was in large part due to the black pilots who never gave up.

> "We were fighting two battles. I flew for my parents, for my race, for . . . first-class citizenship, and for my country. We were fighting for the 14 million black Americans back home. We were there to break down barriers, open a few doors, and do a job."
>
> —Joseph P. Gomer, remembering his time as a Tuskegee Airman

On Veterans Day in 2013, Tuskegee Airmen Ivan Ware (left) and Edward Talbert (center) attended a ceremony honoring the Tuskegee Airmen at the African American Civil War Memorial in Washington, D.C.

TIMELINE

1939
Senator Harry S. Truman sponsors a bill allowing black pilots to serve in the Civilian Pilot Training Program.

1941
The United States enters World War II.

1942
The first class of black pilots trained at Tuskegee Institute completes their advanced pilot training and earns their wings from the Army Air Corps.

1943
Black fighter squadrons are sent into combat in Europe.

1945
World War II ends after Germany and Japan surrender.

1948
President Harry S. Truman enacts an executive order to begin desegregation of the U.S. Armed Forces.

1998
Benjamin O. Davis Jr. earns the rank of four-star general.

2008
The Tuskegee Airmen National Historic Site opens in Tuskegee, Alabama.

CRITICAL THINKING USING THE COMMON CORE

1. What two battles were African-American pilots fighting? Why did they have to fight two battles? Use details from the text to support your answer. (Key Ideas and Details)

2. Suppose African-Americans were not allowed to become military pilots during World War II. How do you think this would have affected the outcome of the war? (Integration of Knowledge and Ideas)

3. African-Americans faced racial discrimination and unfair treatment in their own country. Considering this, why do you think they wanted to fight for the United States during World War II? (Text Type and Purposes)

GLOSSARY

alliance (uh-LY-uhnts)—an agreement between nations or groups of people to work together

cadet (kuh-DET)—a military student

commander (kuh-MAN-duhr)—a person who leads a group of people in the armed forces

fraught (FRAWT)—full of something bad or unwanted

froze (FROHZ)—prevented the act of spending money or the withdrawal or exchange of something

ground (GROUND)—to restrict the activity of someone or something

inferior (in-FEER-ee-ur)—lower in rank or status

Jew (JOO)—someone who is descended from the ancient Hebrew tribes of Israel

morale (muh-RAL)—a person or group's feelings or state of mind

Nazi (NOT-see)—a member of the political group that ruled Germany from 1933 to 1945

racism (RAY-siz-uhm)—the belief that one race is better than another race

recruit (ri-KROOT)—a new member of the armed forces

regiment (REJ-uh-muhnt)—a large group of soldiers who fight together as a unit

segregate (SEG-ruh-gate)—to keep people of different races apart in schools and other public places

squadron (SKWAHD-ruhn)—an official military unit

READ MORE

Burgan, Michael. *World War II Pilots: An Interactive History Adventure.* You Choose: World War II. North Mankato, Minn.: Capstone Press, 2013.

Hamilton, John. *War in the Air.* World War II. Edina, Minn.: ABDO, 2012.

Sandler, Martin W. *Why Did the Whole World Go to War?: And Other Questions About World War II.* New York: Sterling Children's Books, 2013.

Shea, John M. *The Tuskegee Airmen.* New York: Gareth Stevens Publishing, 2015.

INTERNET SITES

FactHound offers a safe, fun way to find Internet sites related to this book. All of the sites on FactHound have been researched by our staff.

Here's all you do:
Visit **www.facthound.com**
Type in this code: **9781491448397**

Check out projects, games and lots more at
www.capstonekids.com

INDEX

Adams, E. S., 21
African American Civil War Memorial, 27
Anderson, Charles Alfred, 14
Army Air Corps, 6, 7, 11, 13, 18, 19, 21, 23

"Black Birdmen," 24
bomber planes, 6, 24, 25
By Request (aircraft), 24

Chicago Defender (newspaper), 15
Civilian Pilot Training Program (CPTP), 11, 12, 13, 19

Davis Jr., Benjamin O., 20, 22, 23, 24, 25
Davis Sr., Benjamin O., 25
Distinguished Flying Cross (award), 25

Gomer, Joseph P., 26

Hastie, William H., 21
Hitler, Adolf, 4
Housen, Jack, 21

James, Emory A., 21
Johnson, Rufus R., 21

Marshall, George C., 18

National Association for the Advancement of Colored People (NAACP), 15
99th Fighter Squadron, 18, 19, 20, 24

Old Faithful (aircraft), 10, 11

P-40 fighter planes, 23
Pearl Harbor, Hawaii, 5, 7
Pittsburgh Courier (newspaper), 10, 15, 16
Purnell, Louis, 19
Purple Heart (award), 25

Red Tail Angels, 24
Roosevelt, Eleanor, 14
Roosevelt, Franklin D., 5, 7

Spencer, Chauncey, 10, 11

Talbert, Edward, 27
Truman, Harry S., 11, 12, 26
Tuskegee Airmen National Historic Site, 12, 25
Tuskegee Institute, 12, 13, 14, 18, 19, 20, 21

USS *Arizona*, 5

Vann, Robert, 16
Vultee BT-13 Valiant, 22

Ware, Ivan, 27
White, Dale, 10, 11
Williams, Roderick, 7
World War II, 4, 5, 8, 25, 26